MW01030151

Weekly Reader Books presents

What to do
when your mom or dad says. . .
"MAKE YOUR BREAKFAST
AND LUNCH!"

By
JOY WILT BERRY

Living Skills Press
Fallbrook, California

Weekly Reader Books offers several exciting
card and activity programs. For information,
write to WEEKLY READER BOOKS, P.O. Box 16636,
Columbus, Ohio 43216.

Printed in the United States of America.
Library of Congress Catalog Card Number: 83-080840
ISBN: 0-941510-18-2

Weekly Reader Books edition published by
arrangement with Living Skills Press.

Dear Parents,

"MAKE YOUR OWN BREAKFAST AND LUNCH!" You've probably said that more than once to your children and received a less than enthusiastic response. Has it ever occurred to you that their resistance to your request may come from not knowing **how** to do what you have asked? The assumption that children will automatically know how to fulfill requests is often the cause of much parent-child conflict.

If you expect your children to do something that they are not equipped to do, it is most likely that they will become overwhelmed and anxious while you become frustrated. Both reactions are prime conditions for an argument!

Why not avoid these kinds of encounters? Who needs them? Much of the negative "back and forth" that goes on between you and your children can be avoided by approaching your expectations intelligently.

Fulfilling **any** expectation always begins with knowing how. Skills are required to do any task, no matter what the task may be. These skills must be learned **before** the task can be accomplished. This is a fact of life!

All too often parents have left their children to discover these skills on their own through trial and error over a very long period of time. But why should this be so? You wouldn't give your child a complicated book in the beginning and say, "Teach yourself to read."

My suspicion is that most parents take certain skills so much for granted, they forget that these skills must be taught.

Does this apply to you? If it does, relax because **MAKE YOUR OWN BREAKFAST AND LUNCH** not only helps children, it helps parents survive as well.

3

If you will take the time to go through this book with your child, both of you will learn some very valuable skills. . . skills that will really pay off in the long run.

Some children will be able to read the book and assimilate all the information themselves, but in most cases you'll get better, longer lasting results if you use the "show me how, then let me do it" method. Here's how it works:

Using this book as a guideline

1. Demonstrate how the task should be done by doing it yourself while your child watches.
2. Do the task together or encourage your child to do the task while you watch. (Avoid criticizing and praise anything the child does correctly while you are watching.)
3. Let your child do the task alone.
4. Praise the work and express appreciation for what your child has done.

If you'll take a little bit of time to teach your child the skills needed to fulfill your requests, you'll save yourself a lot of energy in the long haul.

So don't just sit there—do it! And have fun while you're at it. Who knows, doing these nitty-gritty things with your child may give you some of the greatest and most rewarding experiences you'll ever have together.

Sincerely,

Joy Wilt Berry

4

Has your mother or father ever told you to . . .

MAKE YOUR BREAKFAST & LUNCH!

If this sounds familiar to you, you are going to **love** this book because it will tell you exactly how to make your own breakfast and lunch.

BREAKFAST

Breakfast is your first meal of the day and should include—
- a main dish
- one or more side dishes
- a beverage

BREAKFAST MAIN DISH

Your breakfast main dish should contain protein to keep you going strong until lunch. You can be sure of getting some protein if you choose foods containing one or more of the following:

THE
HAT IS
OPTIONAL.

Cold Cereal

Most breakfast cereals that come in boxes are made from oats, corn, rice, or wheat. Try combining two or more kinds of cereal for more flavor and better nutrition.

Hot Cereal

Hot cereal can warm you on a cold morning. Instant hot cereal may be made by pouring hot milk over your favorite boxed cereal (such as shredded wheat).

To make this, heat one cup of milk until it is warm to the touch. Pour the warmed milk over the cereal in the bowl.

Whole grains, such as oats, millet, wheat, and corn, can be made into hot cereal by slowly boiling them in water. Most grains need twice their measure of water to cook them into a mush.

To make whole-grain hot cereal, you will need a—

SAUCEPAN

MEASURING CUP

SPOON

and these ingredients (for 2 or 3 servings):

1 cup rolled oats, millet, corn, or
  a mixture of grains
2 cups water
$\frac{1}{8}$ teaspoon salt

Procedure for making whole-grain hot cereal:

1. Put grain and water into a saucepan and place on the stove.
2. Turn burner on high until grain and water boil.
3. Lower heat and simmer slowly until mixture becomes thick.
4. Remove from stove and turn off burner.
5. Pour the hot cereal into a bowl.

You can make hot cereal the night before if you have a large thermos bottle. Pour one cup of grain (like rolled oats) into the thermos bottle. Add two cups boiling water and screw the thermos cap on tightly. By morning, the grain will have absorbed the water and your hot cereal will be ready to serve. Be sure to rinse out the thermos immediately after serving your cereal.

Flavor your bowl of hot cereal by adding
1 tablespoon brown sugar, honey, molasses, or
pancake syrup.

If you use sugar or honey, you may also want
to add ¼ teaspoon cinnamon and ⅛ teaspoon
nutmeg.

Top your hot cereal with one of the following:

> a pat of butter
> milk or cream
> a scoop of ice cream
> sliced fresh fruit
> nuts or
> dried fruit

I THINK
HE MAY HAVE
OVERDONE IT
A BIT!

Eggs

Eggs are a good main dish for breakfast. One person usually needs 2 eggs.

Scrambled Eggs

To make scrambled eggs, you will need a—

- mixing bowl
- whisk or eggbeater or fork
- frying pan
- spatula

and these ingredients (for 1 serving):

2 eggs
2 tablespoons milk
⅛ teaspoon salt
1 tablespoon margarine

14

Procedure for making scrambled eggs:

1. Crack eggs into a mixing bowl.
2. Add milk and salt.
3. Beat eggs with a whisk, eggbeater, or fork until they are all yellow.
4. Put margarine into the frying pan.
5. Place frying pan on the stove and turn burner to high heat.
6. Pour egg mixture into the pan and leave at high heat for 1 minute.
7. Reduce heat to low.
8. With the spatula, push the setting eggs away from sides of pan toward the center. Keep the eggs broken up, and cook until stiff but still moist.
9. Remove scrambled eggs from stove, and turn off burner.
10. Scoop the scrambled eggs onto your plate.

EGGHEAD.

You may vary your scrambled eggs by adding one of the following to the eggs while they are cooking:

    sliced hot dogs
    sausage
    bacon bits
    sliced luncheon meats

You can also top scrambled eggs with—

    • grated cheese or
    • creamed chipped beef

16

It may be fun for you to make special sandwiches out of scrambled eggs. First, add a slice of cheese to the eggs. Then, put the eggs and cheese—

- between 2 slices of toast, or
- into warm pita bread, or
- onto a warm bun, English muffin, or bagel.

You may also roll scrambled eggs and cheese into a warm flour or corn tortilla.

Hard-boiled Eggs

Hard-boiled eggs are easy to make and provide a quick breakfast-to-go. To make hard-boiled eggs, you will need a—

- saucepan
- measuring spoon

and these ingredients:

2 eggs
cold water
2 tablespoons salt

Procedure for making hard-boiled eggs:

1. Place the 2 eggs into the saucepan.
2. Add cold water until the eggs are covered.
3. Add 2 tablespoons salt. (This will help prevent the eggs from cracking.)
4. Heat water to boiling over medium-high heat.
5. Remove pan from heat and turn off burner.
6. Leave the eggs in the water and cover pan for 22 to 24 minutes.
7. Uncover saucepan and place it in sink.
8. Run cold water in the pan.

To peel hard-boiled eggs:

1. Tap the shell on a hard surface to crack it.
2. Roll the egg between your hands to loosen the shell.
3. Hold it under cold water as you peel it.

You can eat boiled eggs plain, or you may do one of the following —

- Slice the eggs. Put the egg slices on toast and sprinkle bacon bits on top.
- Chop the eggs. Add 1 tablespoon mayonnaise, ½ teaspoon vinegar (optional), ½ teaspoon sugar (optional) and ⅛ teaspoon salt to the chopped eggs. Mix well. Then spread the mixture on bread, toast, or an English muffin.
- If you do not eat boiled eggs immediately after they are cooked, refrigerate them. They will stay fresh in the refrigerator for up to 7 days. A penciled "X" on the shell will alert you that the egg is hard-boiled. However, you can always test a hard-boiled egg by spinning it: a cooked egg in the shell will spin like a top; an uncooked egg in the shell will barely spin.

Pancakes, Waffles, and French Toast

Pancakes are a breakfast main dish that may be enriched with other good things. Pancakes can be made from a packaged mix following its own directions or from flour, eggs, and milk.

Plain Pancakes

You will need a—

- griddle
- small bowl
- large bowl
- wire whisk or electric mixer
- measuring cup
- measuring spoons
- spatula
- pastry brush

and these ingredients (for 7 or 8 pancakes):

1 cup flour
1 teaspoon baking powder
½ teaspoon baking soda
½ teaspoon salt
1 egg
½ to ¾ cup milk or buttermilk
2 tablespoons cooking oil
1 tablespoon butter or margarine, melted

Note: The amount of milk you use will determine how thick the pancakes are. To make your pancakes thinner, add a little more milk to the batter. To make them thicker, use less milk.

Procedure for making pancakes:

1. Mix the flour, baking powder, soda, and salt together in the large bowl.
2. Break the egg into the small bowl and beat it until it is yellow.
3. Add the milk and oil to the beaten egg, and mix well.
4. Stir the wet mixture into the dry mixture until all of the ingredients are wet. Do not overbeat.
5. Using a pastry brush, grease a hot griddle. (The griddle is hot enough to cook pancakes when a few drops of water sprinkled on the pan jump around.)
6. Pour ¼ cup of the batter onto the griddle for each pancake.
7. Cook each pancake until bubbles appear on its surface.
8. Turn the pancake over with a spatula.
9. Lift the edge of the pancake to see if it is golden brown.
10. Remove the pancake from the griddle. Turn off heat source.

You may vary pancakes by adding extra ingredients to the pancake batter.

- For apple pancakes, add 2 cups grated unpeeled apples, 2 tablespoons, sugar and 2 tablespoons lemon juice.
- For banana pancakes, add 1 cup mashed ripe bananas, 1 tablespoon lemon juice, and 2 tablespoons sugar.
- For blueberry, strawberry, or blackberry pancakes, add 2 tablespoons sugar to the batter, then gently fold in 1 cup fresh, washed fruit. If you use canned berries, strain them before adding.
- Dried fruit, such as raisins, chopped dates, or trail mix may also be added to the batter.

Waffles

You can also make waffles out of pancake batter by adding 2 additional tablespoons oil, and cooking the batter in a waffle iron.

NO, YOU FOOL! NOT THAT KIND OF IRON.

You may top your pancakes or waffles with one or more of the following:

butter

pancake syrup

honey

jam or jelly

molasses

sour cream or whipped cream,
    mixed with fruit

crushed berries in their own juice

applesauce

cheese spread

25

French Toast

French toast is similar to pancakes. Thus, the toppings you use on pancakes may also be used on French toast.

You will need a—

- griddle
- small bowl
- fork
- pastry brush
- pancake turner

and these ingredients (for 2 or 3 servings):

2 eggs

½ cup milk

¼ teaspoon salt

6 slices day-old French bread, or any sandwich bread

1 tablespoon butter or margarine, melted

Procedure for making French toast:

1. Heat the griddle over medium heat, or set electric griddle at 275°F (190°C).
2. Beat the eggs, milk, and salt in a bowl with a fork until blended.
3. With the pastry brush, grease the hot griddle with butter or margarine.
4. Dip 6 slices of bread, one at a time, into the egg mixture.
5. Cook the bread on the griddle for about 4 minutes on one side, or until golden brown. Then, turn the bread and cook on the other side for about 4 minutes until brown. Serve with syrup, jam, flavored yogurt, or powdered sugar.

BREAKFAST SIDE DISHES

Fruit

Fruit is a wonderful side dish.

You may use frozen, canned, dried, or fresh fruit.

If you slice or peel fresh fruit, keep it from turning brown by pouring a citrus juice over it (orange juice, lemon juice, or lime juice).

Bread Products

Bread, rolls, muffins, and bagels are good side dishes, especially when they are warmed or toasted.

- One way to warm rolls, muffins, or bagels is to place them in a brown paper bag, then thoroughly wet the outside of the bag with water. Place the bag into a 350° F (180°C) oven for approximately 15 minutes. (This process will warm the rolls, muffins, or bagels without drying them out.)
- To make cinnamon toast, butter a slice of hot toast, then sprinkle cinnamon sugar on the buttered surface. Cinnamon sugar may be made by mixing ½ cup sugar with 2 teaspoons cinnamon. Use only a tablespoonful at a time.

29

BREAKFAST BEVERAGES

Any fruit or vegetable juice is a good breakfast beverage.

Milk is also a good beverage to drink for breakfast. It may be served hot or cold, plain or flavored.

Hot chocolate may be made by heating milk to which chocolate flavoring has been added.

It is good to have an instant hot chocolate mix on hand for the times you run out of juice and/or milk.

Instant Hot Chocolate Mix

Mix together:

> 6 to 8 oz. jar of nondairy creamer
> 1 lb. package of sweetened ground chocolate or
> sweetened instant cocoa
> 1 lb. 9 oz. size package of instant milk

Store in an airtight container until needed. Add 2 to 3 heaping teaspoons to a cup of boiling water. Add a peppermint stick, marshmallow, or whipped cream for an added treat.

Blender Breakfast

A blender can combine your main dish, side dish, and beverage into one glass. A blender breakfast usually includes—

- a raw egg or protein powder (main dish)
- fruit (side dish)
- milk or fruit juice (beverage)

Eye Opener

Break an egg into the blender. Add a glass of orange juice, 2 tablespoons honey, and 1 banana cut into chunks. Blend until smooth.

Egg Nog

Break an egg into the blender. Add one cup milk, one tablespoon honey, and $1/2$ teaspoon vanilla. Blend until smooth.

Thick Shake

You will need—

• a blender

and these ingredients:

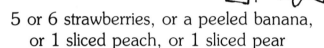

5 or 6 strawberries, or a peeled banana,
  or 1 sliced peach, or 1 sliced pear

1/2 cup cottage cheese, ice cream, or
  yogurt

2 tablespoon honey

1/3 cup cold milk

Procedure for making a thick shake:

1. Put the fruit and cottage cheese (yogurt or ice cream) into a blender, cover, and blend until the mixture is smooth.
2. Turn blender off.
3. Add the milk and honey, cover, and blend until smooth. (If it's too thick, add a little more milk.)
4. Pour into a tall glass.

Here are other things you can eat for breakfast—

- Baked beans sweetened with brown sugar, honey, molasses, or pancake syrup.
- Yogurt or cottage cheese topped with fruit, bran, granola, or nuts.
- Half a cantaloupe filled with yogurt or a scoop of cottage cheese.
- One cup cottage cheese flavored with 1 teaspoon sugar, $\frac{1}{4}$ teaspoon cinnamon, and $\frac{1}{8}$ teaspoon nutmeg.
- Bagel and cream cheese.
- Apple or pear slices with slices of cheese.
- Toast with peanut butter, honey, and sliced bananas.

THESE ARE ALL GREAT BREAKFAST IDEAS, BUT DON'T TRY THEM ALL AT ONCE.

LUNCH

Lunch is a midday meal you may have to eat away from home. If you pack a lunch to take with you, you will need—

- a main dish
- one or more side dishes
- a beverage

LUNCH MAIN DISH

Leftovers make good main dishes for lunch. Check your refrigerator for—

- pizza
- cooked chicken or turkey
- cooked ham or beef

Other main-dish suggestions include—

Armenian string cheese
(sometimes called "rope cheese")

a container of yogurt

cottage cheese and fruit

beef jerky

sliced meat wrapped around a pickle or
chunk of cheese

chunks of food fastened together with
toothpicks (such as chunks of meat,
cheese, olives, pickles, or cherry
tomatoes)

crackers and cheese

hard-boiled eggs

peanuts

Sandwiches

All sandwiches are made with some kind of bread. The bread is usually filled with a protein food, then folded over or topped with a second piece of bread.

Breads that may be used for sandwiches include—

- "regular" bread (preferably whole grain)
- buns
- pita bread
- tortillas
- bagels

Sandwiches may be filled with—

- peanut butter and either honey, jelly, raisins, or banana slices
- cream cheese and either sliced olives or chopped walnuts
- sliced cheese
- sliced meat

You can make a cheese or meat sandwich more interesting if you add one or more of the following—

- mayonnaise, mustard, and/or catsup
- lettuce leaves
- alfalfa or bean sprouts
- sliced tomatoes
- sliced pickles or pickle relish

Sandwich Fillings

You could make a different sandwich every day of the month and still have new ideas for good combinations. There are many different kinds of breads to choose from today, so be adventurous and try different ones each time you buy a new loaf. The fillings, too, may be as varied as your imagination. Here are a few suggestions:

Tuna Salad

Drain one 7-ounce can of tuna. Mix the tuna with ¼ cup mayonnaise, 1 tablespoon mustard, and 1 teaspoon lemon juice. If you like, you may also add ½ cup chopped black olives and/or 2 tablespoons pickle relish.

Chicken Salad

For chicken salad, use the recipe for tuna salad, only add 1 cup of chopped cooked chicken instead of tuna.

Egg Salad

See recipe on page 20.

Cheese Spreads

Add ½ cup grated cheese and 1 tablespoon mayonnaise to 1 cup tuna *or* chicken *or* egg salad. Spread the mix on a bun or between 2 slices of bread. (Pita bread or tortillas may also be used.)

Italian Cheese Spread

Mix together: ¾ pound grated cheddar cheese, 1 small can tomato sauce, 1 small can chopped black olives, ½ cup chopped green bell peppers, ½ package of spaghetti seasoning.
Spread the mix on a bun or between 2 slices of bread. (Pita bread or tortillas may also be used.)

Cheese-spread sandwiches are especially good when they are wrapped in foil, heated in a 350°F (180°C) oven for 15 minutes, and served hot.

LUNCH SIDE DISHES

Vegetables are a nutritious addition to any lunch.

Celery Boats

Wash some celery stalks. Cut off the leafy parts of the stalks. Cut the celery into short pieces about as long as your finger. Spread the celery stalks with peanut butter, or soft cheese spread, or cottage cheese. Sprinkle with raisins or pieces of chopped unpeeled apple.

Veggie Sticks

Veggie sticks may be made with carrots, zucchini, celery, and cucumbers. Wash the vegetables, then cut them into short, narrow strips.

Veggie Flowers

Veggie flowers may be made with broccoli and cauliflower. Wash the raw vegetables, then break them into bite-sized pieces.

Veggie sticks and flowers are especially good when served with Dill Dip.

Dill Dip

Mix together ⅔ cup sour cream, ⅔ cup mayonnaise, 1 tablespoon dill weed, 1 tablespoon ground onion, 1 to 2 teaspoons Beau Monde seasoning, and 1 tablespoon chopped parsley.

WE'RE PRETTY VERSATILE.

Fruit

Fruit is an important part of our daily diet, and some fruit should be eaten every day. You may use—

- dried fruit (including fruit "leather")
- canned fruit
- fresh fruit (squeeze lemon juice over cut fresh fruit to keep it from turning brown)

Apple slices may be served with slices of cheese, or may be spread with peanut butter.

Trail Mix

You can make your own trail mix by adding a mixture of dried fruits to a handful of nuts and seeds and handfuls of your favorite cereal combinations. Toss all ingredients together. Store in an airtight jar.

Chips

Chips made with potatoes or corn are a nice addition to a lunch. However, they should not replace fresh vegetables and/or fruit.

LUNCH BEVERAGES

A thermos bottle can keep a beverage hot or cold for hours.

It is best to carry dairy products in a thermos so they won't spoil.

If you will not be using a thermos, you can still have a cold beverage.

Cold Juice

Freeze small containers of juice. Pack them in your lunch while they are still frozen. The juice will thaw by lunchtime and be cold.

Chocolate Milk

Put 4 tablespoons instant lowfat milk with 1 tablespoon sweetened instant cocoa into a plastic bag. Pack an empty plastic cup and a plastic spoon or popsicle stick in your lunch. To make the chocolate milk, put the powdered mixture into the glass first, add *cold* water, and stir until the chocolate milk is smooth.

TO WRAP A SANDWICH

1. Tear off a sheet of waxed paper 3 times the length of the sandwich.
2. Lay the paper flat.
3. Put the sandwich in the center of the paper.
4. Bring the top and bottom of the waxed paper together and roll it down to the sandwich.
5. Fold the sides of the waxed paper into points.
6. Tuck the pointed sides of the waxed paper under the sandwich.
7. For extra protection, put the wrapped sandwich into a plastic bag or wrap it in foil.

When you pack your lunch, make sure each item is wrapped or is in its own container.

Fresh fruits, like apples, bananas, and oranges are fine wrapped in their own skins.

Other food items may be wrapped in one of the following —

- plastic sandwich bags
- recycled plastic bags
- aluminum foil
- waxed paper sandwich bags
- waxed paper
- plastic wrap

Some foods pack better when they are in containers. Some containers you may wish to use are —

- plastic bags
- recycled plastic yogurt, cheese, or ice cream containers
- baby-food jars with lids
- small tins
- plastic containers designed for lunch boxes

Be sure to include a napkin with your lunch. Pack extra items, like a plastic spoon, saltshaker, or straw when they are needed.

STINK SMELL YiCK OOH!

PUTTING MILK OR ANY LIQUID IN A BAG ISN'T A VERY GOOD IDEA! PHEW!

THE END of not knowing how to make your own breakfast and lunch.